hello

Vancouver

GLC SILVER BURDETT
PUBLISHERS

ELMA SCHEMENAUER

Canada Rainbow Series
Cities

© 1986 GLC Publishers Limited
    115 Nugget Avenue
    Agincourt, Ontario M1S 3B1

Canadian Cataloguing in Publication Data
Schemenauer, Elma.
  Hello Vancouver

(Canada rainbow series)
For use in schools.
Includes index.
ISBN 0-88874-262-2 (bound). — ISBN 0-88874-246-0 (pbk.). —
ISBN 0-88874-269-X (set, bound). — ISBN 0-88874-267-3
(set, pbk.)

1. Vancouver (B.C.) — Juvenile literature.
I. Title. II. Series.

FC3847.33.S33 1986   j971.1'33   C85-099815-8
F1089.5.V22S33 1986

The Author
Elma Schemenauer is originally from Saskatchewan, and is presently living in Ontario. She has taught school in Saskatchewan and Nova Scotia, and has written a number of educational books for children.

Project Editor & Photo Research: *Deborah Lonergan*
Permissions Editor: *Estelle McGurk*
Design & Art Direction: *Holly Fisher & Associates*
Manuscript Reviewer: *Alice Tiles*
Printed & Bound in Canada by: *Friesen Printers Ltd., Altona, Manitoba*

CREDITS
Cover Photo: Hugo Redivo/Hot Shots; Courtesy of the British Columbia Provincial Museum, Victoria, British Columbia, pg. 13; Department of Regional Industrial Expansion photo, pgs. 6, 8, 9, 10, 11, 17, 18, 19, 22, 23, 24, 25, 27, 29; J. G. Graphics, pg 7; SSC Photocentre — photo by Beverly Olandt, pg. 20; SSC Photocentre — photo by Ted Grant, pg. 21; SSC Photocentre — photo by Brian King, pg. 26; SSC Photocentre — photo by T.W. Kitchin, pg. 28; Courtesy Vancouver City Archives, pgs. 14, 15, 16.

hello
Vancouver

Contents

Whoosh! A black and white killer whale shoots out of the water. Killer whales are stars of the show at the Vancouver **Aquarium.** In Vancouver you can watch whales in the morning and ski in the afternoon. Or you can mountain climb in the morning, watch **hang gliders** dive off cliffs at lunch, and swim in the afternoon. Vancouver is a jewel of a city nestled between the mountains and the Pacific Ocean. It's a great place for outdoor living. It has the mildest **climate** of any mainland Canadian city.

Killer whales wait to greet you at the Vancouver Aquarium in Stanley Park.

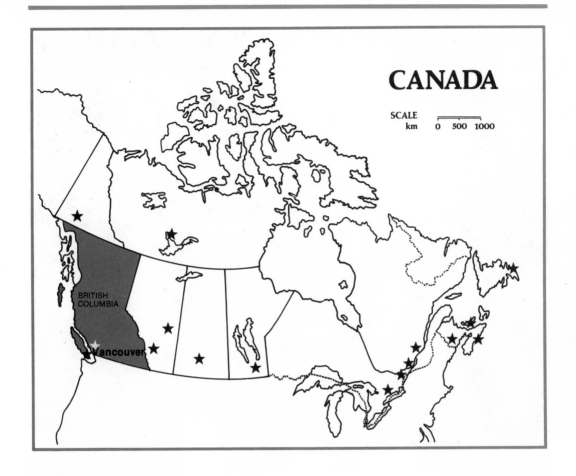

CANADA

SCALE
km   0   500   1000

BRITISH
COLUMBIA

Vancouver

"The City by the Sea" is what people often call Vancouver.
It is on the misty coastline along the southwest edge of
mainland British Columbia. On the city's sea side are the blue
waters of the **Strait** of Georgia. On its land side are the Fraser
Valley and the Coastal Mountains.

   Vancouver is one of North America's most important
Pacific sea ports. With well over a million people, it is also
Canada's third largest city.

Totem poles in Stanley Park, downtown Vancouver's "green thumb."

It looks like a giant hand reaching out into the Strait of Georgia. That is the wide peninsula on which the main part of Vancouver is built. Along the **peninsula's** southern edge flows a narrow branch of the Fraser River. Along its northern edge is Burrard **Inlet.** (In Vancouver, people are never far from water!)

A large "thumb" sticks up from the "hand of land" on which the main city is built. On and around this thumb of land is downtown Vancouver. In a way it is a "green thumb" because beautiful Stanley Park is at the end of it.

Killer whales wait to greet you in Stanley Park. People flock to the park's Aquarium to see them. Aquarium visitors can also meet a funny character called Bee Bop Beluga.

But people don't go to Stanley Park just to visit the Aquarium. The park is within jogging distance of the city's many West End apartment buildings. Many apartment dwellers — and others — go to Stanley Park to bike, roller skate, play **cricket,** golf, and listen to outdoor concerts. Children can ride a tiny railway in the park. It chugs around a duck-filled pond, miner's hut, and model Native Canadian village.

Meet Bee Bop Beluga! Real live beluga whales live at the Vancouver Aquarium, too.

"I'll meet you at Georgia and Burrard." That's one of the main street corners in downtown Vancouver. Among the interesting nearby buildings are the Orpheum Theatre, the Vancouver Art Gallery, and the Queen Elizabeth Theatre. Special highlights are the domed sports stadium and the jewel-like Expo Centre. They are at BC Place, site of the 1986 World **Exposition,** called Expo 86.

Across False Creek from BC Place is Granville Island. At its colourful market you can buy everything from a whole salmon, to a basket of BC peaches, to a slab of walnut fudge made right before your eyes.

The Expo 86 site overlooks False Creek. A highlight at Expo is "the world's largest hockey stick."

What interesting things could you do in Vancouver's Chinatown?

Where can you see the "World's Thinnest Office Building?" It's on Pender Street in downtown Vancouver's Chinatown. Called the Sam Kee building, it is only 1.8 m wide. But it stands two storeys high!

In Chinatown you can also see phone booths with **pagoda** roofs, buy Chinese toys, have tea in a Chinese teahouse, and eat **bean curd** cakes and almond cookies. Vancouver people are proud of their interesting Chinatown.

They are also proud of Gastown. This is a colourful area of shops and restaurants not far from Chinatown.

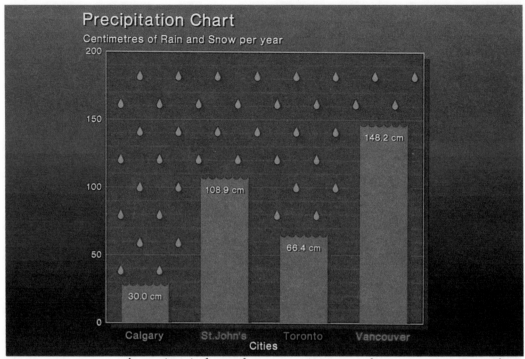

Precipitation Chart

Centimetres of Rain and Snow per year

Vancouver	148.2 cm
St.John's	108.9 cm
Toronto	66.4 cm
Calgary	30.0 cm

Cities

As moist air from the ocean rises over the mountains, it cools and rains on Vancouver. Most other Canadian cities receive less rain.

Vancouver children seldom get a chance to build snow forts. To play in the snow, they usually have to go to the mountains. In the mountains, the snow often stays all year. In the city, however, the weather is always mild. Average January temperatures are around 3°C. Average July readings are a pleasant 18°C.

It rains a lot though. Vancouver gets about 150 cm of "liquid sunshine" a year. The people don't mind too much. They know the rain keeps their grass and forests green. By March their city will be carpeted with yellow daffodils, while most other Canadians are still **slogging** through slush and snow.

Long ago, only Native people made their homes in the area now known as Vancouver. They were Coast Salish Indians. These people lived in large cedar houses. They gathered roots and berries, and fished for salmon.

The first Europeans to see the area may well have been Spaniards. However, the **credit** usually goes to English sea captain George Vancouver. In 1792 Captain Vancouver explored and mapped the mild misty coastline. He noted its heavy **stands** of rain-forest timber.

Cedar houses at a Coast Salish village about 1866. How did these people obtain their food?

Timber-r-r-r! By the 1860s there was a mill settlement in what is now downtown Vancouver. Saws squealed. Huge trees groaned and crashed into the underbrush. Grunting ox teams dragged the forest giants to the **sawmill.**

Soon "Gassy" Jack Deighton arrived on the scene. Jack was a big jolly man. His nickname came from his love of "gassing," or **spinning** stories. Gassy Jack soon saw what the mill workers wanted — a tavern! He built one. It quickly became the centre of a community known as Gastown. People who didn't like the name Gastown called it Granville.

Gastown in the early days. People often met to talk in the shade of the big maple at the left.

On the right, first CPR train to reach Vancouver. What an exciting day!

The Canadian Pacific Railway was a great "ribbon of steel." Built during the 1880s, it linked British Columbia with the rest of Canada. Railway manager William Van Horne chose Gastown, or Granville, as the CPR's western end. He sent a land agent to lay out streets for a city. He also changed the community's name. "Vancouver it shall be," said Van Horne firmly.

Vancouver became a city in April 1886. A month later, a raging forest fire burned it to the ground. Showing their tough pioneer spirit, Vancouverites immediately began rebuilding their city.

By the year after the fire, Vancouver had nearly 100 new stores and businesses. The population was over 8000.

This population grew rapidly. In the late 1890s, check-shirted gold seekers **mushed** their dogs through the streets on their way to the Klondike gold fields. A number of the gold seekers later came back to settle in Vancouver. As the years passed, the city became a centre for the great natural wealth of its province — timber, fish, furs, and gold and other metals. Since World War II, Vancouver, like many other Canadian cities, has received a flood of new people from many lands. They have given the city an exciting international flavour.

A store on Vancouver's Cordova Street, 1898. It sold boots, sleeping bags, and other supplies to Klondike gold seekers.

Vancouver from the air. Where are some of the communities that make up the Greater Vancouver Regional District?

What began as a mill town quickly grew into a large **urban** area. It is now called the Greater Vancouver Regional District. (That's GVRD for short!)

Included are 17 communities. One of these is the main city of Vancouver. North of it across Burrard Inlet are North and West Vancouver. South of it are Richmond, Delta, and White Rock. To the east are Burnaby, New Westminster, and other communities along the Fraser Valley. One special community among the 17 is the University Endowment Lands. This area is the site of the University of British Columbia, western Canada's largest university.

Model of Vancouver's exciting new Canada Place. Planners build models to help people see how new buildings will affect the surrounding area.

Voters in the 17 GVRD communities elect directors. These directors meet to decide on matters affecting the whole urban area. Among such matters are: use of land, hospital planning, parks, water supply, air pollution, and mosquito control.

Each separate community within the GVRD also has its own government. In the main city of Vancouver, this is a Council made up of a mayor and 10 aldermen.

Vancouver City Council meets in City Hall. This is a solid-looking white building. A statue of Captain George Vancouver guards the north entrance. A ship's bell rings to signal the beginning of Council meetings. The Council deals with matters affecting the main city of Vancouver.

Unlike most Canadian cities, Vancouver has political **parties** in its city government. Each party has different ideas about what is best for the city. For instance, one party may think Vancouver should have more factories. Another party may disagree because factories can pollute the air. Each party tries to convince the voters of its ideas.

Vancouver City Hall. How is Vancouver's city government different from most other Canadian city governments?

Not long ago the Hotel Vancouver asked its staff how many different languages they spoke. Among them, they could speak a total of 21 different languages!

Vancouver is quite an international city. Its first non-Native settlers were mostly English and Scottish. People with a British background still make up about half the population. But there are also large groups who trace their roots to Germany, China, Italy, India, Scandinavia, and Greece. Some tourist booklets call Vancouver "The World in a City."

Putting up signs during Vancouver's Italian Day celebrations. Why is Vancouver called "The World in a City?"

Lacrosse, often called "The Fastest Game on Two Feet." It was first played by Native Canadians.

As we have seen, Chinatown is a showcase for the city's Chinese **culture.** Robson Street could be called a showcase of European cultures, especially German. You can hear polka music on Robson Street. You can eat tasty sausages and pastries. You can buy newspapers printed in many languages. People often call it Robson *Strasse* (German for *street*).

Totem poles in Stanley Park remind people of the city's Native Canadian beginnings. So does the popular game of **lacrosse.** Games between the New Westminster Salmonbellies and the Vancouver Burrards are always exciting.

Inside Vancouver's new domed stadium, site of many major sports events.

Vancouverites also enjoy many other sports. They like to watch Vancouver Canucks hockey games, and B.C. Lions football games. In July the city holds its Sea Festival. The main event is the Bathtub Race. Entering the race are powered bathtubs from many countries. They set out from Nanaimo, sloshing across the wide Strait of Georgia towards Vancouver.

Then there's the Polar Bear Swim. This takes place on New Year's Day. A few daring souls brave a dip in the bone-chilling waters of English Bay. B-r-r-r!

Daring — maybe that is one good word to describe Vancouverites. At least that's the way they appear to people from other large Canadian cities. Vancouverites seem more willing to take chances, to try risky new ways of doing things.

At the same time, many people in Vancouver seem more relaxed than those in other large Canadian cities. They seem to strike a happy balance between work and enjoying life in the beautiful outdoors.

Pleasure boats in Vancouver harbour. The city offers people many opportunities to enjoy life in the beautiful outdoors.

Vancouver's new system of overhead trains helps move people around the city quickly and easily.

Most Vancouver people have to cross the water at least twice a day. Many of their city's communities are divided by water. To get from one to the other, Vancouverites drive or walk across the city's more than twenty bridges.

To get from downtown Vancouver to North and West Vancouver, people often take the Seabus. This is a system of ferries. At either end, the bright orange ferries connect with the city's bus system. But the transportation talk of the town nowadays is a brand new system of overhead trains. It is one of Vancouver's big projects for Expo 86.

As in the past, Vancouver still gets a lot of its wealth from B.C.'s rich **natural resources.** Timber is one of these. Many people in and near Vancouver work at jobs connected with it. For instance, they are loggers, sawmill workers, and lumber yard workers. Salmon is another leading resource. Many Vancouver area people are salmon fishermen or have jobs connected with salmon fishing.

The government tries to make sure the timber and salmon resources will always be there. Forest workers plant new trees to replace those chopped down. Salmon hatcheries hatch baby salmon to replace those that have been caught.

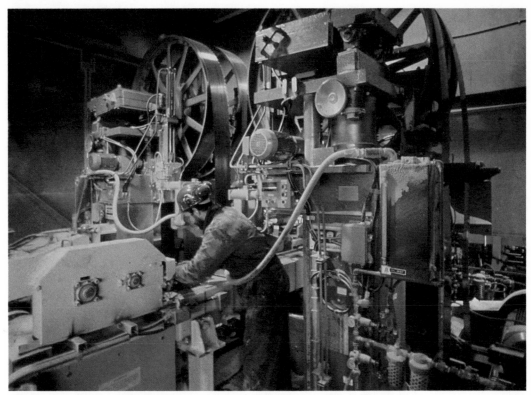

Many people in and near Vancouver work in jobs connected with the timber industry. What other jobs do they do?

A lot of Saskatchewan wheat goes out through the port of Vancouver. So does a lot of Alberta beef. So do timber and precious metals from B.C.'s mountain mines. Vancouver is an important link between Canada and the rest of the world. Ships from Vancouver carry Canadian trade goods to Japan and other Pacific countries. As a result, many Vancouver people have jobs connected with the harbour, and with ships and shipping.

Vancouver is B.C.'s money and business centre. This means a number of Vancouverites also work in banks, real estate offices, and other business places.

Vancouver's harbour. What are some of the things that are shipped through this port?

Meeting "Gassy" Jack in Vancouver's Gastown. Why do so many tourists visit the city?

Known as one of the most beautiful cities in the world, Vancouver **attracts** a lot of tourists. A number of Vancouver people have jobs taking care of tourists.

One thing that Vancouver does not have is a lot of **manufacturing.** Not many goods are made there. Of course, the city does have rich natural resources to depend on. However, when natural resource products do not sell well, many Vancouver area people lose their jobs. There are few jobs in factories for them to fall back on.

*Feeding a
swan in
Stanley Park.
What do some
Vancouverites
fear factories
might do to
their beautiful
natural set-
ting?*

On the other hand, what if a lot of new factories did start in
the Vancouver area? What might that do to the city's natural
setting? Would some of its most beautiful views be blocked or
spoiled? What about pollution?

Finding enough housing for people is another Vancouver
puzzle. The city's urban communities keep spreading eastward
into the Fraser Valley. But this is the province's richest
farmland. Should it be swallowed up by a sea of houses? The
government has already taken some steps to prevent this.
Perhaps it will need to take more in the future.

In 1979 a group of Vancouverites came up with one exciting solution to the housing problem. They created Sea Village next to Granville Island. It is a village of floating homes! **Residents** pay city taxes. They are hooked up to city services such as telephones and electricity. Their rowboats are "parked" outside, so they can easily go shopping.

That kind of daring and imagination help make Vancouver an exciting city. It's a great place to live. No doubt the city's government and people will find ways to keep it like that in the future.

Sea Village at Granville Island. What is one Vancouver problem that Sea Village helps to solve?

Glossary

aquarium — An area or building where living fish and other water animals are shown (p. 6).

attracts — Draws to itself; gains the interest of (p. 27).

bean curd — A food made from "milk" obtained from soybeans. Bean curd is smooth, and has a mild flavour (p. 11).

climate — The kind of weather conditions a place has over a period of years (p. 6).

credit — The honour or praise for some deed (p. 13).

cricket — An outdoor game played by two teams of 11 players each. They score points by batting balls and running to wickets, or goals (p. 9).

culture — The way of living and/or the artistic products of a group of people. Also fineness of manners, taste, and feelings (p. 21).

exposition — A large public show or exhibition (p. 10).

hang glider A kite-like craft that has no motor, but stays in the air by gliding on air currents. Usually one or two people hang from one hang glider (p. 6).

inlet — A narrow strip of water running into a coastline or between islands; a small bay (p. 8).

lacrosse — A game usually played by two teams of 12 players. A player carries and passes the lacrosse ball using a stick having a pouch made with strips of leather (p. 21).

mushed — Journeyed by dog sled, usually while urging the dogs along by shouting commands at them (p. 16).

manufacturing — The producing or making of things, especially by machine (p. 27).

natural resource — A material found in nature and used by people. For example, lumber, water, and gold are all natural resources (p. 25).

pagoda — A temple having many storeys, which form a tower. Most often found in China, Japan, and India (p. 11).

party — A group of people who want and work towards the same kind of government or action (p. 19).

peninsula — An area of land extending out into water from a mainland. A peninsula has water almost all around it (p. 8).

resident — A person living in a place (p. 29).

sawmill — A building or business where machines saw timber into boards, planks, and so on (p. 14).

slogging — Plodding heavily (p. 12).

spinning — Telling, or making up and telling (stories) (p. 14).

stand — A grove; a group; a standing growth of plants (p. 13).

strait — A narrow channel of water linking two larger bodies of water (p. 7).

urban — Referring to a city or cities (p. 17).

Index